T0334936

# LARK
# APPRENTICE

## New Issues Poetry & Prose

| | |
|---|---|
| Editor | Herbert Scott |
| Copy Editors | Eric Hansen, Jonathan Pugh |
| Reader | Cody Todd |
| Assistants to the Editor | Rebecca Beech, Lynnea Page, Marianne E. Swierenga |
| Business Manager | Michele McLaughlin |
| Fiscal Officer | Marilyn Rowe |

New Issues Poetry & Prose
The College of Arts and Sciences
Western Michigan University
Kalamazoo, MI 49008

First Edition, 2004.

ISBN                1-930974-41-8
Library of Congress Cataloging-in-Publication Data:
Mathias, Louise
Lark Apprentice/Louise Mathias
Library of Congress Control Number: 2003113930

| | |
|---|---|
| Art Director | Tricia Hennessy |
| Designer | Sara Broderick |
| Production Manager | Paul Sizer |
| | The Design Center, Department of Art |
| | College of Fine Arts |
| | Western Michigan University |

# LARK
## APPRENTICE

**LOUISE MATHIAS**

New Issues

WESTERN MICHIGAN UNIVERSITY

If the lark is lyric, the work of a lark's apprentice is to aid and re-learn the lyric as experience itself. This philosophical adept is an apprentice who inhabits the solitude of words themselves. She—or it—would marry undoing with doing; she would not only soothe but would unsoothe, would honor the difficulty of saying before not-saying. In a series of delicately crafted intensities, Mathias fiercely shows the conundrum of thinking and feeling.

—Brenda Hillman, judge's statement

*for D.D.L.*

# Contents

# III.

## Acknowledgments

Thanks to the editors of the following publications, in which some of these poems originally appeared:

*Blackbird:* "Autumn Sequester," "Blue Agnostic"

*Boulevard:* "Quarantine"

*Crazyhorse:* "Quandary"

*Denver Quarterly:* "Desert Flux," "In California, Everything Has An Aura"

*Epoch:* "Equinox"

*Green Mountains Review:* "Mute Swan"

*Hunger Mountain:* "Agapornis Personata (Masked Love Birds)," "Heretic," "Lark Apprentice"

*The Journal:* "Mutilation," "White Moves"

*Meridian:* "Boxing"

*Prairie Schooner:* "Hula," "Fielding," "'Sexual,' He Said," "O Zone"

*Red Rock Review:* "A Brief Nostalgia," "Catastrophic Theories," "The Bones Explain"

*Salt Hill:* "Drift"

*Shade:* "Blind Alley," "Subterranean," "Wingspan"

*Slope:* "According to Experts," "Conjugal," "Ghost Limb"

*Quarterly West:* "Not Traveling," "Recognition"

Thanks to the following individuals whose comments and/or encouragement helped shape this book: Lisa Gluskin, Stephen Massimillia, Stephanie Kartalopoulous, David St. John, Heather McHugh, David Dodd Lee

# I.

*(Everywhere we've been is darkly wooded.)*

## Desert Flux

Here is a lesson in discard. After the fire
Bird "A" continues to hover

on her scientific twig (on the *shadow*
of twig—)

Bird "B" is flying in circles. Ruptured hoop
of the sun's corona. What led

you here? The wrecking moon;
the vast,

tight passage of impasse. Light that is bridal
& in the end, a nuisance.

How to fathom

the sequence of the body; its trial
& veil.

## Bird On a Wire

How long we had waited to fall.
Grief illuminates, gathers as she goes.
A woman's back. Sudden. Embroidered

with scars. But scars are coquettish, like roses
& whimsy. They draw attention to themselves.
Don't talk to the air so much, she's God's informant.

Thus, she's viral.

## Blue Agnostic

Why so long with your disbelief?
I see several ships, they are moving toward us,

their sails are tattered, but they tack & ride
each swell.

At night the sea is cast, spider-silted. The flinty
underbelly of a ship. Did I imagine

that blue distemper? That crashing,
inextinguishable loss—

The frequency's fixed. Array. Array.
& those who sent it

will never know its true expense to us.

## Drift

When I say *the politics of this town*
*are not mine,* I mean
they slap stucco on its flaws, paint
their women into corners, set the house
on fire.

If there is no region, why
the philosophical map with just one city?
*House* is an emotional structure,
grim and vertical

with rooms that lead nowhere, that atmosphere
and twist.

When they say *hitchhike, Hitchcock,*
I'm supposed to call to mind
the murderous trees,

rootless and brooding for roots,
belligerent and dealing.

## Lure

It's the old dilemma. Nude, we're all

the same, diminished & fetal.
(A tern fell out of the sky. I made
an imprint in the lining of my dress.)

Do nights have pleats? I was the rifler

between them. Some hands
turn up so pale they're really thistles . . .
There's no irony there (anise).

No changing of the guard in Navajo White.

Just our bodies, smart
with complications. And our mouths;
pink halos of effort

in the black apparatus of night.

## Subterranean

To move in a woman, he says, is to move
underneath

that place on the map where the body gives in
& the mind shuts off (long gasp

that sounds like sorrow). It's no crime to want to live

where the sun beats down
with the conviction of a drug

& it isn't a crime to love

the pitch-black curve of the ever-elusive tunnel,
the apocalyptic white of her thigh—

the swing of hair, long past *jasmine* and
on its way to *blithe*.

Long ago I also reached to touch a woman's hair.
It scared me half

to death. Its rustling, oceanic
dreaming.

## Body of Wish

I know my body is quotidian:
the rise & fall of me

is the rise & fall of anyone else.

But in the dream I am plural/specific.

Forest slaughtered. Forest sprung
of green, green wish.

You came to me in that dream. A chemical leak
where *windfall* meets *need.*

Sometimes we play the *would you love me* game.

By the time we're done, you're a paraplegic _____.
& I'm a _____, wheeling you around

with one eye, willing.


*


Lawless thing, where is your capital city?
(Your heartbreak mouth—

the terse, twin cities of your hands.)

Have you always been literal/winter?

## Blind Alley

Lilies; those charming imposters.
In the adamantine daze

of the low-slung sun, they tried
to convince you.

You always fell in love with man-made things—

The future hovered,
in taut, industrial darkness. The world at large

stood up, in dumb applause.

How they beckoned; relentless, forgiving.
The sound of another summer,

bottoming out.

## Partial Eclipse

Not happiness, exactly. Who,
this late in the game, was equipped for that?

We were given the sky. Obsidian stretch
of native skin, it sustains itself—

We were given a day. Then (shockingly) the next.
The Good Book said

we could learn to live on this earth, where
nothing was sacred. & the moon, in her

occasional failings, was merely pretty.

## Net Zero

It was removal did you in. My own unbiblical
heart just sat & watched. Handful

of ashes, the fields all furious, white. On every coast
I know

the waves outdo the brides—Someone sings

a song about gradient living, the half-obscured
stars. I stole

from the nest. It was simple. Remote

& spinal,
this was the country where I lived.

## A Brief Nostalgia

Whatever crystalline force was in you
I've scattered like ashes, like telephone

calls thrown out in the early years. But
what was the point? Love fell

from the strangest places (balconies,
rafters), dead on arrival. Much like

your long shaft of hair, the toughening
stars. Why insist that the life cut short

is worthy of drama? What of
the longer life, the lush, lush

line brimming with prim green
promise? What if the proverbial

night, its angular presence, in time
could be softened, made right?

## Stark Heaven

Each winter has its inopulent day.
In the field where lost souls gathered, vibrato
through the trees, impressionistic—

a faulty realistic. I believed that faith
was a box. (That once we were in it,
the lid would snap shut

with a calm & a clasp.) We'd escape

to our own interior gaze, which grows
in one direction & with the taut
precision of violin strings.

Now, a bleating school of winter trees.
*What is this new deliberation on my hands?*

# Equinox

In the rational world, we had no use
for atmosphere

& arias. We had heard
of the plight

of stars,
but would never forgive.

Who lent them their oriental
drama?

Who told the lilies
they had a say in love?

Scaffolding builds, until it is tough
as the weather. (When I said

the world was
damaged, I meant damned.)

I meant, lay beside me, my darling
objector.

Play me a breeze, in the late, late
language

of hush.

## Wingspan

*That's the trouble with love,* she thinks,
*it's parenthetical.*

Her one true vein is in her upper thigh, no map

he can follow. Notice her exhale;
it's a little bit longer than his. Still,

he gets her down to what she wants: her whittled list.

Once, she licked his Christ-like inner wrists
with her own brand of un-

restraint, akin to terror. She knows one thing
and likes to think it, hard:

the birds evicted

from their troubled path of flight. His lupine kiss.

# II.

*(For a time, even the trees were inconsolable.)*

## Lark Apprentice

In the bleak & beautiful country of childhood,
there is a very last nerve

and you can get on it. (Note: it easily tires
& isn't built

for years of withstanding much.)
When a relative died, I developed an earache: high

ringing note in a cathedral of ice.
The operation (mine) was a success. Still,

I think it's prairie, deep in there, some place
you couldn't bear to wander.

(Though I'd hold your hand. We'd bring some snacks
and a cheap, disposable camera.)

When the film was developed, we'd appear
as rising ghosts.

## Boxing

*(Something grave)*
            *(in any man's face)*

The whites of his eyes
blooming like floodlights, the oxblood gloves

                    *(vehemence)*
            *(poppies)*

organic as womb. A brief & tender moment, she wipes
his upper lip, his nostrils flare

*(incandescence)*
            *(the paraffin light)*

and then this hothouse waltz, this bruising, this cash.
What does a mouth sound like, collapsing?

*(teeth loosening)*
                *(a woman's strand of pearls*
*come undone)*

## Conjugal

(Everywhere we've been is darkly wooded.)

When did so many trees
spring up? How did the city
grow hair?

*Quick, count her fingers & toes. Make sure*
*there aren't too many—*

A classic dream
is the lyrical dream:
the small blue alcove
above a prisoner's head
is falling/failing
(as only sky knows how)

These choices—these un-choices. How to
eradicate their source?

*The car was leaving when I got there.*
*It was just a woman's leg.*
*Her leg.*

Ephemera—(the art
of collecting) disposable
goods. Very *magpie*
of you, darling,
very

## Quandary

All night I flew the dark recess of God's mind.
It was arranged like Iowa fields—

not a damn thing missing.
You ask how I survived.

I lived on a message, broad light
at the end of the world.

Words, they have so much in common with departure,

the clouds elliptical & nervous.
Why translate? It's just a revolving door.

"Chill wind" has seven
components. One is loss.

## Context

He wants to bind my wrists with ribbons, please. Preferably
    scarlet, as in
a woman scorned. Face down in the snow,

that's what you get, hitch-
hiker.

Rain on rain,
base coat for a slippery night. & the blade:
what's so sexy about it? Blood is a ribbon.
Her heart-shaped ass is the device. I could say
a little more, but I won't. An inverted heart
is still a heart, you know.

Pure as grief before it is stricken.

## Ghost Limb

Not death, but a version of it. Quixotic nurses
visit at night, like angels, but harder. Question:

sounds like *refrigerator*. Answer: *respirator*.
My family tree cut short, more of a shrub.

The mother country's breath smells foreign, like babies.
What to wear? What to wear? A net of stars

and then a cape of smog.

## Placebo Effect

I have two wives, he says.
*Blanca y Negra.*

They speak an invented language. Alternate nights
they slip in my bed, although

my landlord bars them. They've dined on my breath
so long, we dream the identical dream:

the war of the rat. The year of missing teeth.
The industrious faces of hundreds

of Chinese children.

## In California, Everything Has An Aura

*Potato:* penultimate fist
*Authority:* the sky with her bag of supplies

*Filigree:* second child of the smallest flower
*Sangria:* the Island of Dance

*April:* summer's torn-off dress—
*Poverty:* slim resurrection

*Noon:* one steely, steely eye
*Garment:* the weather, of course

*Storage:* the heart's cold solution
*Colt:* gesture masked as chestnut loss.

## Heretic

Beyond the tarnishing landscape, infidel sky—
it wasn't the fear of living I feared

but the black

automotive sun, its rigorous blinking. In the city,
this sort of thing is crucial: waking up to a battery cry

both piercing & convincing

(that's not the soft bird leaking through
plantation shutters)

God's little sidekicks: resilience & death. With someone else
I became a mini-death, a murderee.

In order to reason with any aplomb, I *had* to leave.
The other me was in the corner having visions.

It was of concern, but not "The Problem"
the lab coats said.

## Catastrophic Theories

"I'm studying the structure
of shadows," he said,
gesturing in the air. "Your umbra,
your penumbra—

if I were you and you
were me, I'd cover
you completely." (He was
handsome

in that dusty, college way,
so I moved in close, ripe
for the eclipse.)
He said

"Last night I dreamt of love,
and it was a woman, and I
was loved." "Love's a lot
like astronomy,"

I said. "The role of heat—
the preternatural death
of stars." He shook
his head.

"They're polar opposites,"
he said. "Science demands
you explain the inexplicable.
Love

demands you turn a fistful
of weeds into a wild
bouquet from a distant
planet."

## Fait Accompli

Sage, I had no policy to guide me, save
the thinning lull of poor girls' shoulders, save

their pocketless holes. Sage, I had no bliss;
I had more hands than I had angels. Sage,

you hapless virtue, I'd no magnifying
glass. No adulation. No miracle of sleep.

Sage, I had no questions, save
your answers. Sage, those dark-tailed birds?

*They fill the streets.*

## Platform 20

. . . & your skin
was a field

I had walked in as a child. I bit
your shoulder, watched

the space around the scar.

A season like summer, I guess. Clouds

picking up their skirts
in an effort to leave.

We're not to be blamed
for the way

our blood instructs us.

## Autumn Sequester

For a time, even the trees were inconsolable.
They, who had carved a life from structure—

building on root. Strange
how years later they come into focus. Wind picks

at their offspring & carries away

with little fanfare, but a flutter. This small green
island *is*

the past. I remember
so little except the axis turning. I didn't know her,

but I kept her grief in my sleeve.

Talisman. Verdict. On a small green island
death gathers

with the upstart force of physics. Fervor
& further. Was it just to see the crying?

We could manage so little. Even to speak

would belie
the massive heart.

# III.

*(But the sum of her parts was such a brutal equation.)*

## "Sexual," He Said

". . . meaning, I feel

them *here.*" We were looking at peonies again,
their swollen heads almost glib with pink—

a lustrous, Spanish sort of finish.

(A netted ballgown, an antique, dusty
kiss.) I could feel myself

beginning to object. Becoming
objectionable, & yet

you get so tired
of your own conjugations, your Freudian luggage

multiplying in its sleep.

He was just *admiring their fullness* &

in a parallel country, a woman wanted
a man like he was breath.

It was everywhere around us. The world
was *florid.*

& who was I to disobey this tidal hint?

## O Zone

What a beautiful way to keep you out—
At the center of a maze, a tight white flower
imagined herself into being,

as though it were a profession, no, a curse.
Tonight's moon is all disguise, a stagger of white.
Small wonder that we were in love

with her gauzy arrival . . .

## She Tries to Convince Herself That She, In Fact, Owns Her Body

If not, then who does? Not God—
he's shown no interest in years. Absent

father, I've scanned the fingerprints he left,
his electric *maybe* that still hinges

on the quiet edge of night. I never imagined
such a deft melancholia; that lavender

mood would suit you so well. Nor
this costume of bones (this skin you wear

is such a low-cut dress). If this
were a formal affair, Revisionist History 101,

you'd be a taffeta drone. You'd shop
at the Store of Faith, the Store of Yes.

Those luxe, luxe landings where *Impossible,
Darling* was not

the only verdict left.

## Atrophy, Transatlantic-Style

*I am well,* she writes to me now—

                                  *long time, no love.*

Memory boards a virtual plane; makes a move
to resurrect her. The bird

in her face, her chestnut hair, her wired limbs—

The past (the grown-ups told us)
belongs in the past. But in the land

of not-forgotten things,
it curls like a fist.

They drew the curtains.
A muffled light

snuck in.

## Duet In Airport Blue

Lately, on my own spiral staircase. Nothing above

& nothing below. Some words
fell out of the side of my mouth but I learned

to disguise them. Little orphan words

that no one wants. Dear God,
if it's just conviction you're after, belief & dis-belief

are one. The dark shock of a stranger's eyes
blew through like a comet. Perennial,

exotic. The color of an ancient,
seething mud.

## Elemental

I. Earth on Fire

How presumptuous you are
to land your little red plane

next to mine. Your rumblings
are all about sex, which interests

me little, except in brief
mid-Spring. Your one hot note

is frankly exhausting, sure,
sure, you're stripping your

way through medical school.
Me? I'm a woman who kicks

while my beauty is stolen.


II. Air on Fire

Oh god, I love your dress!
Of course, we'll never dance,

my blue & gaseous horizon
leading only up, your lateral

rumba less skyward than
rubied. Go ahead, burn my feet!

I haven't felt them in years.
In the end, it's a tragic

equation: your vague glow,
my impossible stairs.

## Eyeful

There is a shell inside a shell. No, that is too
easy. Love's location

is approximate & pink. A woman raised
her eyebrow, that is all.

Every month has a shadow affair.
June's: a little swarm. It rustles,

like a skirt. If you fell too long
you'd catch—

(a bit of silk)
catch wind of it—

## Mute Swan

(no trumpet) & (no keeper). Save the loyal
spotlight on the water . . . The moon

is a fool; keeps shedding her miracle light.
Your name is a lie; when the bird-heart

collapses, there's a sound like any
mother's: *death on wheels.*

But keep your lie. Your hospital coat.
Your economy bite. Your icy, circular dance—

no partner, no aim. (In another poem, dear,
you'd mate for life.) How jealousy

moves—wants to snap the S of your neck
for being so lovely.

Brief feather. Transient engine. Circular bloom.

## Agapornis Personata (Masked Love Birds)

It's their use of color that gets me: languid
& brazen, when they should be shy.

Why is the tip of *green* so desperately shocking?
Filament wings, in all their jaunty

dare . . . I asked the man what he wanted for the pair.
*I want that they continue,* he said. *& you name*

*them yin & yang.* & this one here, so sherbet
& tender, as if bleached poppies could up & fly.

In their distinctive chatter, odd endearments:
Petal Wing, let me map your town

of downy kisses. Sugar-beak, pack up your weekend
bag of blue joy.

## Mutilation

Take the word itself on a date,
out of its native country, smuggled
in brown parcel paper or led like a cow, into a field
that won't matter. Undress it. Command it

to walk like a woman (down

on its hands and knees). The pedestrian
now seems exotic. Zoological.
A romantic if distant creature, almost pretty
enough to name your daughter
after.

## The Bones Explain

We didn't know you would look like a war:
holed up in your apartment all Fall

with only a measuring tape and a bag of grapes,
cutting grapes in half and licking knives.

Rather, we thought you'd become
a swan-like girl from the Eastern Seaboard,

all ponytail and pearls, and we'd lay,
aristocratic and smooth, in your delicate

décolleté. It's your mother's fault, not ours.
She always said we were big. We wanted to prove

her wrong and look, we did. Just look at your wrists.
Small as sparrows, lithe as wintering wrens.

## Twine

Did you forget what's lush? You trailed it for years.
It clipped at your heels. Dear, if you're honest
it ran you. & when, after all this time, you put
your hands on your own life
& felt it rage, it had the humid air
they'd call nostalgia . . . Though,
you'd been in the mire so long,
never seen a face like his; ripped
from the side of God. Like a breath

believed in.

## White Moves

The game was of obliteration. Fog lifting

her delicate dress & *nada*
underneath. (& the *nada* was female.) Cavity.
Clinic.

      Is white the color of nothing? Non-color. Un-
color, standoffish color throwing opaque

zeros in her mouth? The color of *lack,* the color
of *flee,* the color of *no*

           *I must be going.* The color of space
on ice, froth
on air, deafness stuffed with cotton wool, clouds

with no direction.

## Hula

I welcome you with my hands
                              (that end in orchids)
                    (impossible necklace)
(gratitude)

            I welcome you with my skin
                  (not so) (exotic)
(much like your wife's)
                        (nightgown) (of shadows)

                I welcome you with my skirts
(multiple) (fragrant)
                      (inside them)
                              (small animals live)

I welcome you with my breasts
                              (coconut)
(armor)

              I welcome you with my eyes
        (the left one)
                    (predictor)
                              (the right one)

(mute)

## Quarantine

In her latest dream, the telephone had grown
enormous. She had to climb over it to feed the dog

yet couldn't dial out. The local news
talked of bloodhounds, the scent of a woman,

the human equivalent of a cat stuck up a tree. The threat
of tornadoes (or any natural disaster) in time grows

redundant.  She started to pine for a man
with a smell on his hands. In his ambient, nasal

voice he'd talk of the city: that slim magician.
That taxicab confession. That wispy rumor of air.

## Bottomlands

My brief sojourn into that death, it did not matter.
The purity of landscape (how it fails).

I picked this silver willow
by the lake, a kind of slender proof

that life still grows . . .
My worst affair was with the past, he had

my back. Such a sheen to that horizon—
though,

you understand, this was a form of trespass
too.

## Cottage Industry

I was trying to make
a system for light,

an accounting department
for the volatile heart:

her payables. Her
receivables. I was trying

to balance the light
with the dark, unwrap

the tight box
of contradiction

[god]

dismantle the
obstacle

[fact]

I was trying to vary—
though mostly

deep inside
my dress.

I was trying to catch
the slow dance

of virtue. For years
I traipsed

through that Hydrangea
mess.

## Showy, Irregular Flowers

& then he broke her fingers
        one by one,
                or so the story goes

& I put down
        my novel in despair . . .
                this fourth summer in a row

of women on the verge.
        I've never known
                the other side of *verge*—

though I can well imagine
        a grim, unfashionable place
                much like this yard

(its concrete slab & showy,
        irregular flowers). Exhibit A:
                this year's blushing brides—

Peonies! Peonies! (Their pleated,
        petticoat heads that multiply
                & whirr with oh, such pink

& sudden, certain death!)

## According to Experts

Mother Earth is an ever-reducing planet. Via Internet, airport,
a canopy of nerves & roaming

charges. Your faux-faux cousin gives you a new Italian toy:
"Expatriate-in-the-Box." All wound up,

he cries "Bella, Bella." *I prefer romaine,* one aunt
says, her arms and legs dangling

from her dress like popsicle sticks, all the cream sucked
off by Aunt #2, who in direct contrast

to the earth is ever-expanding. In years past, I used to *try*
to sign my name with festive flourish;

take up space. These days I'm a one-question woman.
What's Italian for *brevity, grief?*

## Barren

Fear, I suppose. Not of the distance, tiled
with stars, but the sun of return.

Her blonde charisma through the clouds
a curious hatching. (Lilt

in the throat of the larks, county
of rushes). How summer lights

each small misgiving's face. My sweet
unchildren spin in their snubbed orbit;

I said quit. Sometimes I envy a man;
the way a woman's nipples down his back

become erasers . . .

## Not Traveling

She was a fragile bride, afraid of catching
too much color. Crimson:
a devastating picnic. Khaki: a long-
delayed plane. Teal: an impetuous
rental car.

So they stayed home. It was just their luck,
he said, when the plane he wished he
had been on went down, somewhere
off the coast of Costa Rica. They lay in bed, kicking
like babies

while people died. He slowly pulled
one white sock off and then the other.
Raised them above his head like sorry flags.
When she was a kid you couldn't have
paid her

in Boston Baked Beans to watch the news.
She knew there was nothing worth knowing
she couldn't invent herself. He'd been
an industrious child, and still was,
criminal, even—

traveling over what she had long considered
the private counties of her body. Telling her
they were small and not unlike others
he had seen. Tugging at the foliage.
Renaming things.

## Fielding

(But the sum of her parts was such a brutal equation.)

Couldn't you take a part at a time, the derisive
left earlobe, the trail

                that *hot* left behind? I

spell the woman who time left by, I've been spelling
her nightly. Hers is the scalp, shorn

or luscious. I'd like to describe

the lilt of her chin,
but the woman, the woman won't lilt.

                    Call me crazy, I like
what time does, a slow-warming trend

that moves through the East,
our pasts becoming child brides

(small & utter)

## Spinner

In the end, he wanted to hold me. I was
the thing that could be held—

my nipple in his mouth; carnelian, fragile.
Outside

the critical field, the cottony

sling of clouds, we try
to trace the shape of ringing bells.

*If it isn't for you, my love, my tongue
is a coffin.*

The calloused outskirts
of his hands; the way the left one

moved, then locked
inside me.

## Recognition

I used to crave
the hot fiction of a beautiful girl,
life handed to her, like some prize.
In her youth she tore
at the wrapping some,
but nothing could hide her lovely,
her body like a shocking dessert.

Now I want my heroine less tragic:
more notable for what she lacks
than what she is,
a quiet name that does not hammer
of arty haircuts and stilettos.
By her twenties she has settled
into something secretarial,
with runs in her stockings,
eating yogurt at her desk.

It comforts me to think of her,
balancing cups of coffee,
walking the long halls of her life
in dress after forgiving dress.

photo by J.S. Huston

Louise Mathias was born in 1975 in Bedford, England, and grew up in England and Los Angeles. Her poems have appeared in journals such as *Boulevard, Prairie Schooner, Quarterly West* and *Epoch*. She currently lives in Long Beach, California.

# New Issues Poetry & Prose

Editor, Herbert Scott

Vito Aiuto, *Self-Portrait as Jerry Quarry*
James Armstrong, *Monument In A Summer Hat*
Claire Bateman, *Clumsy*
Michael Burkard, *Pennsylvania Collection Agency*
Christopher Bursk, *Ovid at Fifteen*
Anthony Butts, *Fifth Season*
Anthony Butts, *Little Low Heaven*
Kevin Cantwell, *Something Black in the Green Part of Your Eye*
Gladys Cardiff, *A Bare Unpainted Table*
Kevin Clark, *In the Evening of No Warning*
Cynie Cory, *American Girl*
Jim Daniels, *Night with Drive-By Shooting Stars*
Joseph Featherstone, *Brace's Cove*
Lisa Fishman, *The Deep Heart's Core Is a Suitcase*
Robert Grunst, *The Smallest Bird in North America*
Paul Guest, *The Resurrection of the Body and the Ruin of the World*
Robert Haight, *Emergences and Spinner Falls*
Mark Halperin, *Time as Distance*
Myronn Hardy, *Approaching the Center*
Brian Henry, *Graft*
Edward Haworth Hoeppner, *Rain Through High Windows*
Cynthia Hogue, *Flux*
Christine Hume, *Alaskaphrenia*
Janet Kauffman, *Rot* (fiction)
Josie Kearns, *New Numbers*
Maurice Kilwein Guevara, *Autobiography of So-and-so: Poems in Prose*
Ruth Ellen Kocher, *When the Moon Knows You're Wandering*
Ruth Ellen Kocher, *One Girl Babylon*
Gerry LaFemina, *The Window Facing Winter*
Steve Langan, *Freezing*
Lance Larsen, *Erasable Walls*
David Dodd Lee, *Abrupt Rural*
David Dodd Lee, *Downsides of Fish Culture*

M.L. Liebler, *The Moon a Box*

Deanne Lundin, *The Ginseng Hunter's Notebook*

Joy Manesiotis, *They Sing to Her Bones*

Sarah Mangold, *Household Mechanics*

Gail Martin, *The Hourglass Heart*

David Marlatt, *A Hog Slaughtering Woman*

Louise Mathias, *Lark Apprentice*

Gretchen Mattox, *Buddha Box*

Gretchen Mattox, *Goodnight Architecture*

Paula McLain, *Less of Her*

Sarah Messer, *Bandit Letters*

Malena Mörling, *Ocean Avenue*

Julie Moulds, *The Woman with a Cubed Head*

Gerald Murnane, *The Plains* (fiction)

Marsha de la O, *Black Hope*

C. Mikal Oness, *Water Becomes Bone*

Elizabeth Powell, *The Republic of Self*

Margaret Rabb, *Granite Dives*

Rebecca Reynolds, *Daughter of the Hangnail; The Bovine Two-Step*

Martha Rhodes, *Perfect Disappearance*

Beth Roberts, *Brief Moral History in Blue*

John Rybicki, *Traveling at High Speeds* (expanded second edition)

Mary Ann Samyn, *Inside the Yellow Dress*

Ever Saskya, *The Porch is a Journey Different From the House*

Mark Scott, *Tactile Values*

Martha Serpas, *Côte Blanche*

Diane Seuss-Brakeman, *It Blows You Hollow*

Elaine Sexton, *Sleuth*

Marc Sheehan, *Greatest Hits*

Sarah Jane Smith, *No Thanks—and Other Stories* (fiction)

Phillip Sterling, *Mutual Shores*

Angela Sorby, *Distance Learning*

Russell Thorburn, *Approximate Desire*

Rodney Torreson, *A Breathable Light*

Robert VanderMolen, *Breath*

Martin Walls, *Small Human Detail in Care of National Trust*

Patricia Jabbeh Wesley, *Before the Palm Could Bloom: Poems of Africa*